The Poetical Alphabetical Book

By Heather Reilly

© 2014 by Heather Reilly

All rights reserved. The book's author retains sole copyright to all intellectual contributions to this book, including but not limited to text and images.

No part of this publication may be reproduced, stored in a retrieval system, or transmitted in any form or by any means, electronic, mechanical, photocopying, recording, or otherwise, without written permission from the author.

ISBN: 978-0-9919367-6-2

For Marc and Megan's
future mini Cooper.

This book is also dedicated to the staff at the Stepping Stones program in Whitbourne. Thank you for creating such welcoming and complete programs for the children in our communities.

 is an apple aloft in a tree,

 is for baby, a wee buzzing bee.

C is for **c**atnip that **c**razy **c**ats love,

 is the **d**aylight **Da**d's **d**og sees above.

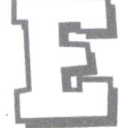 is an **e**lephant **e**normous and gr**e**y,

's the **f**air tooth **f**airy **f**lying this way.

 is a **g**a**gg**le of **g**eese **g**oing by,

 is a **h**amburger and **h**ot french fry.

I is an igloo for Inuit friends,

J 's the jade jungle a jaguar defends.

 is a **k**angaroo **k**i**ck**ing his foot,

L is a **l**lama, his **l**ong woo**l l**ike soot.

M is a **m**arvelous **mumm**er that sings,

 is the **n**ew year the **n**umber **on**e brings.

O is the **o**strich **o**utside **o**n the plains,

 is for **p**arachutes **p**lunging from **p**lanes.

Q's a **q**uick **q**uarrel that isn't so **q**uiet,

R's a **r**ed **r**ibbon, a **r**oyal will buy it!

 is a **s**lithering **s**erpent all green,

 is **t**wo **t**angoing **t**ur**t**les I've seen.

 's an **u**mbrella **u**nder cold splashing rain,

 is the ***v**room* when I **v**acuum a stain.

W's the **w**inter **w**ith **w**ind, ice, and sno**w**,

 is e**x**amining bones **x**-rays show.

 is a **y**ak, that **y**awned next to a **y**urt,

Z's a **ze**bra **ze**stfully juggling dessert.

All of these letters make sounds in each word,

Sound out your name now, which ones have you heard?

Activities to Help Children Learn the Alphabet

Children are often first introduced to the alphabet by the popular song. At a very young age, children can learn to copy or sing the song from rote, but that doesn't give them any concrete connection to what letters look like, or what they mean on paper.

To help them understand that the words to the song they love has meaning in language, reading and writing, there are more than a few activities you can expose your child to. As the caregiver, parent, or teacher, you will have to decide when your child is ready for each of the following suggestions. Keep in mind, that if they "don't get" one of the games, they can still benefit from experimenting with them, and the exposure they get from seeing the letters.

These games and activities can be revisited time and time again until the child is confident in their skills.

Play Dough Letters

This is a great activity for children of all ages. The following is a non-toxic and very easy to make recipe for home-made play dough:

1 cup flour (I use all purpose)
½ cup salt
2 tbsp cream of tartar
1 tbsp oil (I use olive oil)
1 cup water (added gradually as needed)
food colouring

Mix first four ingredients in a pan over medium heat. Add water gradually until the dough clumps together in a lump. Remove from heat, add four or five drops of the food colouring colour of your choice, and knead until the colour is uniform. Store in a sealable container (I use an old butter container) at room temperature. It will keep for months.
Apply this to the alphabet using letter guides (see next page).

Letter Guides

Draw the capital letter "A" on a piece of paper. If you can draw block letters or bubble letters so there is a space inside, all the better. Give your child the play dough and see if they can cover or fill the letter with it.

As the child progresses, add lower case letters to the mix, and eventually give them just the play dough, with no letter guide to see if they can make the letter on their own.

This activity can be repeated using different mediums besides play dough: Q-tips, popsicle sticks, pipe cleaners, and cooked spaghetti can also be used on letter guides to help teach them what lines, curves and angles are used to form the letters.

Letter guides can also be used to do gluing with various things like dry rice, cereal, sparkles, confetti and more! Do a different letter of the alphabet each day, and hang them on the wall in order as they dry.

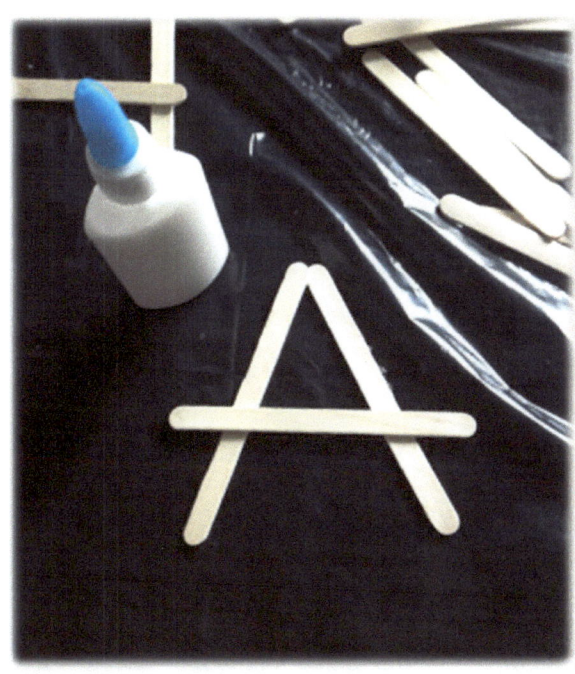

White Boards

White boards can be purchased very inexpensively at the local dollar store. An alternative, if one isn't available, is to laminate a piece of white paper and use a dry erase marker on that. It works almost as well, but erasing isn't always complete.

Every day, write your child a daily note focusing on a new letter of the alphabet. Begin with examples of short 2-3 letter words that start with the day's letter. Read the letter together (or read it out loud to younger children). After, let the child have the dry-erase marker to try to write letters on the white board too. They may trace, they may copy, or they may doodle. All of these experiences are steps to begin making their own first letters.

We have a giant white board at our house, and it is used every day. As a side note, Mr.Clean Magic Erasers will take dry erase markers off of everything, including walls and furniture.

Good morning Connor and Lily,

Today's letter is the letter "E".
At the end of a word, E can sound like "ee", or it can be silent as in me, tree, rake, and bake.
We hope you have a day full of glee!
Love,
Mommy and Daddy.

(The reading word for today is (see).)

I see a cat.

Fill your child's life with things that allow them to see letters and words.

Letter magnets for the fridge are wonderful, especially when paired with sight word cards for them to try to copy. These letters also stick very well to cookie sheets and baking pans. Write a short word, (like cat or dog), on a small piece of paper and put it in the pan. Put the magnetic letters they need to make the word in the pan too, but in a mixed up order. Let them try to make the word by covering up the letters on the paper with the magnets. For more advanced children, let your child try to take the right letters right from the fridge to make the word in the pan.

Alphabet or nursery rhyme posters on their bedroom walls will be discovered and taken in on all those nights when the kids aren't quite tired, or in the mornings when they wake. Books at bed time or any time are wonderful too. Let the child watch you follow the words with your finger as you read, and they will usually start reading that way too.

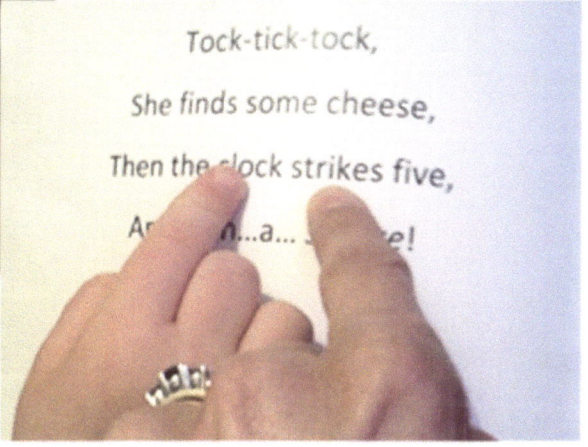

Other books by Heather Reilly:

Novels:

Binding of the Almatraek Book I: *Knight's Surrender*
Binding of the Almatraek Book II: *Noble Pursuit*

Children's:

The Tree and the Sun
Tock-Tick-Tock, the Mouse and the Clock

Upcoming books:

Binding of the Almatraek Book III: *Enchanted Page*
The Words We See: Kindergarten Sight Words on the Rock

Learn more about the author and her books at:
www.reillybooks.com

Titles are also available at amazon.com,
and novels on ebook at smashwords.7-com

www.ingramcontent.com/pod-product-compliance
Lightning Source LLC
Chambersburg PA
CBHW060802090426
42736CB00002B/130